salmonpoetry

Anchored

Lorna Shaughnessy

salmonpoetry

Published in 2015 by
Salmon Poetry
Cliffs of Moher, County Clare, Ireland
Website: www.salmonpoetry.com
Email: info@salmonpoetry.com

ISBN 978-1-910669-22-8

COVER PHOTOGRAPHY:
Martina Gardiner Photography – www.martinagardinerphotography.com
COVER DESIGN & TYPESETTING: Siobhán Hutson
Printed in Ireland by Sprint Print

Salmon Poetry gratefully acknowledges the support of
The Arts Council / An Chomhairle Ealaoín

For my sisters, Miriam and Angela

CONTENTS

Acknowledgements

My thanks to the editors and publishers of the following publications in which versions of these poems were first published: *Clifden 35* (Anthology), *Cyphers*, *Over the Edge: The First Ten Years, An anthology of fiction and poetry* (Salmon Poetry, 2014), *Skylight 47*, *Prometeo*, *The Galway Review*, *The SHOp*.

Nothing is sudden. Not an explosion — planned, timed, wired carefully — not the burst door. Just as the earth invisibly prepares its cataclysm, so history is the gradual instant.

'Fugitive Pieces' ANNE MICHAELS

Crystal

The blower adds breath to heat,
turns and blows within the mould
until he finds precise form.
Molten glass vibrates.

It takes ten years
to learn how deep you can cut
before the glass shatters,
how deep you have to go
to catch the light.

Mistakes pile up
waiting for the furnace,
a second chance,
instability anchored
by the weight of lead.

The Limestone Bowl

Scant winter rains are not enough
to flood Carran's limestone bowl.
No swans this year, but a flock of starlings
that rise in a caligrapher's upward stroke.

The turlough is empty but my cup is full
of gifts to mark another year:
a pair of hands steady at the wheel,
the yellow sun of a freshly-baked cake.

The new season enters in the wake of death,
discreetly tip-toeing behind the mourners.
No rain, ice or snow, just the silent thrust
of white tips unobserved until today.

South

The old god has ridden hard all night,
his sweat-flecked steeds straining to clear
the sky of familiar cloud.

We stir into February, squinting
and stunned by unexpected light,
our movements jerky and out of sync,

take our bearings then head south
through the dip and swell of rolling fields
unscarred by winter storms,

saluted by the outstretched limbs
of deep-rooted trees grown slowly
into shapes of steadfast greeting.

Abroad in a smiling, windless land
we sit on a harbour wall to drink tea
and photograph the water's startling blue,

throw stones that break the water's skin
and plunge with the pure compulsion of gravity
to meet the thrumming drag of the current.

The open sea growls but means no harm.
Waves break in caves beneath our feet,
grumbling with the thunder of contained gales.

Looking for Coordinates

'Reality invents me,
I am its legend.'

JORGE GUILLÉN

Morning. The world returns
in the surfaces of things,
outlines that help define
the contours of the self.

Oblivious to my presence
they inhabit the tenuous day
with the shapes and textures
of a world well-crafted.

Sleep-addled eyes
don't quite see them
but feel their frequencies vibrate
beneath half-closed lids.

Soon, the dim gleam of wood
beckons the eyes to look,
the warp and weft of sheets
awaken nerve-endings in the skin.

The sun gifts presence.
Conjured by its rays
solidity settles on the room,
shadows resolve into form.

I look for the morning's coordinates
in the compass of a window,
hoist the blind, open panes wide
to fill the curtains like sails.

The moment becomes a plumb-line
that points to the earth's core.
I can safely raise night's anchor,
push out into the day.

Pickings

Shoes leather-wet in early mushroom-spotting meadow-
walk past spider-gauzed hedges a sticky end for some
swell-berries darkening rusty red to black sloe-
shaded sparrows hedge-busying as September
sun sparks high larksong over fly-crusted cowpats
last flutter-bys float and double dog-tail gate-keepers
wet-nose boots strolling hill-down to hand-scratching
eye-stinging clusters of fruit picked for muslin-staining
drip and thicken-stirred boiling then viscous glug-
pouring into parchment-topped jars
label-dated and snap-lidded jewels
held up to glow in window-slanted light.

Río Tinto

We cannot enter the Roman graveyard.
The gates are padlocked and chained
so we press our faces to the wire,
squint at the skewed angles of mossed stones,
the departed minions of enterprise and empire.

Behind us the mines, where pulleys and sidings
punctuate strata of centuries-old endeavour.
Rock and mineral are bared in russets and ochres
too raw for peopled places. Their cratered wounds
fill with water so deep you could drown there.

Today is Sunday. In the high, hushed
absence of trucks to rumble up the hill
we try to hear beneath the wind,
listen for the sound of stone,
touch the injured past, its fissured heat.

'Apples Sweeten in the Dark'

Life can only be understood going backwards; but it must be lived forwards.

SØREN KIERKEGAARD

Apples Sweeten in the Dark

Growth is silent,
visible only after the event;
the infant's head
larger on the pillow
in the morning.

Aquarium

I knew you were there
long before I saw the blue line,
felt a flutter of seahorse tendrils
against deep red coral inside.
A year ago you dived out of sight,
hormonal weights tied to your feet,
into unfathomable adolescence.

Today we drift through dimly-lit tunnels
of submarine dreams, captivated
by pulsing coral towers, darting neon tetra,
rippling anemones.

For a moment you re-emerge,
break the surface of monosyllabic self
saying 'Look, it's the tree of life',
offer me an arm to link.

Safety drill

Parents should fit their own oxygen masks
before assisting children with theirs.

But what if the apparatus should slip?
What if they catch a glimpse of our fear,
all needy orifice, gaping mouth and nostrils
sucking up the air meant for them,
hands flailing and useless when the loss of oxygen
breaks the link from brain to limb?

Will they observe our terror knowingly,
and with a rueful set to their lips,
a soft shake of the head, will they calmly
take up their own masks, expertly fit them
and after a perfectly safe landing
evacuate the cabin without us?

The Rower

The rower's eyes are fixed on the shore he has left.
He knows where he has come from
and he will not lose sight of it
till the pull of the length of his body
and the full strength of his legs
propel him far upriver to negotiate currents,
steer clear of reed-beds and shallows,
endure the bullying wash of bigger craft.

And when that shore fades to a pale blue line
he alone can divine what's at his back,
the unseen future the river will reveal,
sounding out the rhythm of his heartbeat,
sounding it out in the rhythm of his stroke.

Moving Like Anemones
(Belfast, 1975)

I

I cannot recall if you met me off the school bus
but it was winter, and dark in the Botanic Gardens
as we walked hand in hand to the museum.
Too young for the pub, in a city of few neutral spaces
this was safe, at least, and warm.
The stuffed wolfhound and polar-bear were no strangers,
nor the small turtles that swam across the shallow pool
where we tossed pennies that shattered our reflected faces.
We took the stairs to see the mummy
but I saw nothing, nothing at all, alive
only to the touch of your fingers seeking mine,
moving like anemones in the blind depths.

II

Disco-lights wheeled overhead,
we moved in the dark.
Samba pa ti, a birthday request,
the guitar sang *pa mí, pa ti*
and the world melted away:
the boys who stoned school buses,
the Head Nun's raised eyebrow.

Neither ignorant nor wise,
we had no time to figure out
which caused more offence,
our religions or the four-year gap between us.
I was dizzy with high-altitude drowning,
that mixture of ether and salt,
fourteen and out of my depth.

III

The day was still hot when we stepped
into cool, velvet-draped darkness.
I wore a skirt of my sister's from the year before
that swung inches above cork-wedged sandals.
You were all cheesecloth and love-beads.

I closed my eyes in surrender
to the weight of your arm on my shoulders,
the tentative brush of your fingers
that tingled on my arm, already flushed
by early summer sun.

Outside the cinema I squinted,
strained to adjust to the light
while you stretched your long limbs like a cat.
You were ripe for love and knew it;
I blushed and feared its burning touch.

Sundays

She wore fur to Mass, mink gifted by a sister in America.
The chapel was cold and I pressed close,
writing my name in matt, back-brushed letters
that dissolved in the silky pile of her sleeve.

The real wonders began when she put on her apron
and placed the chicken-gizzards on a plate,
an improvised lesson in biology. I hovered round the sink
of coiling, waxy apple-peel, angling to suck the eye-smarting cores,
steal a sugared slice or two before the tart was sealed.

Or followed my father's call to walk the dog, skipped and prattled
through park gates, climbed onto the stoic, stone lion's back,
ran and kicked leaves till hunger sent me back to the embrace
of Sunday's smell as the kitchen door opened and the cool damp
of my skin and hair met condensation on the windows.

And if grace was never said, it burnished every surface,
banished the creeping unease in adult voices,
the urgent plea to shush that accompanied the news,
restored us in the safety of small rituals and the senses.

The Injured Past

He who comes into equity must come with clean hands.

LATIN MAXIM

Truth exists; only falsehood has to be invented.

GEORGES BRAQUE

Dogged

The injured past comes back like a mangy dog.
It hangs around, infecting my doorstep with its sores
and the smell of neglect, trips me up when I venture out,
circling my legs, ready for the next casual kick.

If I feed it, it'll never go away.
If I ignore it, it'll never leave
but press its scabby skin against the door-pane,
crouch in the corner of my eye, licking its paw,

or cower in the wing-mirror as I drive away
and limp out to meet me when I come back,
loyal and unwelcome as disease.

Uncovered

*'The Truth shall set you free? Maybe. But first
the Truth must be set free.'*
　　WOLE SOYINKA

Facts, like sunlight, reveal the smeared surface of memory's lens,
the dust and detritus in those awkward corners
where we keep the things we didn't want to know.

Other people and their pain crowd those corners
of my comfortable house. Demanding to be noticed
they look me in the eye and ask, now what?

And what am I to say, finding only words
that take me in circles with no clear exit
from a prefix that binds us all to the past?

remorse　　　repentance　　revelation　　　remembrance
　recognition　　remission　　redress　　　　retrieval
reparation　　reconciliation　　restitution　　restoration

Let the facts speak for themselves, perhaps?
Desert the lyric's quest for closure,
the tyranny of the tidy, final
　　　　　　　　　　　line?

The Dark Topography

There is a country known only to the bereaved of that time,
a place not seen through the car windows of passers-by
who know nothing of genealogies of pain,
the dual burden of trying to find out
or trying to forget the truth.

They see only green fields, hedges, villages and farms,
don't know the ruined cottage was abandoned after a shooting,
the new bricks in the corner of a bar were added after a bomb,
the tarmac beneath their wheels poured over blood-stains;
that too many headstones in the cemetery are carved with
    the same dates.

Loaded

Do they talk about their guns, these men,
when they meet in back rooms and empty places?
Or are the swaddled packages never named
for fear the words may leave a forensic trace
imprinted on the air, mingling with musty odours
somewhere between the lips of the speaker
and the uninitiated ears of a listener?

We've seen how they handle them in films:
tentative, respectful, the frontier boy's reverence
as he cradles the stranger's single-action Colt,
beckoned beyond words by its glamour.
Others brisk and efficient, the drive-by hit-men
or assassins crouched at high windows
who do not speak, who silence the act.

What words do they use when they buy a gun?
Does it get technical, the idiom of ballistics,
all rates of fire and target density?
Or does the need to conceal meet braggadocio
with macho acronyms and arcane abbreviations,
macabre codes for experts and aficionados
to flag their knowledge of the finer points of killing?

Forensic

It marks a body for life,
indelible configuration of contours:
arches, tented or plain, with or without a delta,
loops, radial or ulnar, plain or accidental whorls,
peacock's eye and double whorls
only readable to the trained eye.

A cosmos of selves imprinted by secret
secretions of the eccrine and sebaceous glands,
recovered by the simple application
of powder to surface at the scene of the crime
or eerily revealed in laboratories,
photographed and filed.

Five fractions are then applied,
$Ri/Rt + Rr/Rm + Lt/Rp + Lm/Li + Lp/Lr,$
a number for each print assigned.
Calculation narrows the field, helps identify
those who have good reason to hide.
A fingerprint is not an easy thing to lose.

Keeping Time (April 1975)

Sunday night in a quiet, country club.
The door pushes open, a witness sees
the perforated muzzle of a Sterling SMG
and thirty-three bullet-holes penetrate the walls.
There will be no fingerprinting at the scene.

To this day, every Sunday night at the hour of the attack
a daughter locks her doors and draws her curtains
as if the gunmen keep coming, year in, year out,
as if she can still protect him from his own candour,
his open doors.

No-one Saw it Coming (July 1975)

The bushes are burning
but the only voices he hears
are the angels of death.

Fire has spread from the van to the verges.
Deafened by the blast, the bass player
drags himself to the edge of a field.

No-one saw it coming in the dancehall
when men swore as they pushed out past the doorman
and sped into the dark to give the all-clear.

No-one saw it coming when the last set ended,
the band packed up and left or when men in uniform
swung a red lamp on the road.

No-one saw it coming when the van was searched,
the band lined up to give their names and dates of birth
and 'mind the instruments, they're worth a lot of money'.

No-one saw it coming. Two men in uniform
try to slip a bomb in the back.
The blast throws the band clear of the road.

The only voices to come from the burning bushes
are angels of death: the 9mm Luger pistol, a .38 Enfield,
a .45 Colt revolver and the 9mm Sterling SMG.

Shelter (May 1976)

The gun sleeps, snug
in the wall of a milking shed.
Somewhere else on the farm
a cache of explosives, more arms.
When questioned, the farmer says
'A boy left that here five weeks ago'.

Tip-off (June 1976)

Three objects are placed on the interview table: the 9mm Luger pistol, a magazine containing four bullets and a homemade silencer. Insulating tape has been stripped from the silencer in the fingerprint lab.

'Any idea why your prints are on these?'
'No.'

The detective lifts the improvised silencer, a metal tube, fakes a few flashy moves like a drum major.

'You sure about that?'
'Look, one night in the club, a fella asked me for some tape.'
'He asked you for tape?'
'Yeah, I gave him the tape from behind the bar.'
'You gave him the tape.'
'Yeah.'

The detective sighs and replaces the silencer on the table.

'Do you see any tape on this?'
'No.'
'Neither do I. Let's try this again. Have you any idea how your prints got here?'
'They told me you only found them on the tape.'

In a labelled bag in the fingerprint lab, a pallid strip of tape coils like a shed snake-skin.

The Chosen (January 1976)

He thought he'd breathed his last
when they asked his religion
and told him to step forward.
A workmate's hand urged caution
but they hadn't come for him.

'Don't look back', they said
and shoved him on his way.
He staggered down the unlit road
and felt as though his own bones shattered
when they opened fire on the ten left behind.

The Watched Phone

Her son is out there somewhere
the rain beats his jacket seeps through his jeans
runnels of water travel from nape to chin

somewhere out there her son in seeping jacket
beaten from nape to chin
travels through runnels of water

out there the rain seeps nape to chin
water runnels down jeans and jacket
her beaten son is travelling

he seeps through jeans and jacket
runnelling out somewhere
rain beats

water seeps and her son
travels rain-runnelled nape to chin
beaten out

Standing Ovation at 'The Crum'

Mannequins stand patiently in their cells.
Stripped and alone, they are waiting for their clothes.
At last, the walls of Crumlin Road Gaol have dried
and thermostats show favourable conditions
to present antique costumes from the Bolshoi:
peasants, a Tsar, one black swan and one white.

A prison timeline on the wall recalls hardships lived,
not acted, by suffragettes detained a century ago.
A glass case displays a prisoner-poem written after birching.
The afflictions of others hover in the wings,
the blindfolded stumblings of the interned
between lines of baton-armed soldiers and Alsatian dogs.

Now Johnny Cash is piped through the prison gift-shop
that sells T-shirts announcing 'I've been to The Crum';
souvenir carbolic soap in period Victoriana wrapper;
large slabs of 'Jailhouse Choc' and sticks of 'Jailhouse Rock;
posters that advertise an Elvis Tribute Band
'Coming Soon'.

Heritage kitsch offers souvenirs of others' distress,
draws no distinction between the wielder of the birch
and the wielder of the baton. Differences dissolve
in the safe branding of something called 'the past',
bar-coded, price-tagged and available for purchase
in a present that boasts of progress.

So Elvis will come and we'll all sing along
and videos of the Bolshoi will play on a loop
in dehumidified cells and when the music stops
we can stand and applaud, throw roses to the stage,
sell more tickets for the next performance,
the next peace-tour, gift wrapped.

Questions ricochet around memory's stubborn walls.
The mannequins, rigid in their cells, will not dance.

Silt

Grief is the silt swept up in turbulent waters.
It settles in the pit of the stomach
only when the pace of history slows down,

creeping forward imperceptibly,
clogging up clear channels that once ran
from gut to head, gut to heart,

building up a dense sediment of pain
till there's nowhere else the water can go
but outwards, break the levees, overflow.

The Crossing

The word is a tug that trawls
the first line across the river
and hooks it to the other side.

We follow, haul ourselves hand over hand
over fraught currents, dangle perilously
above submerged rocks, tangles of weed.

Vowel over vowel, we move slowly,
taking the pain, taking pains
not to lose a grip of the line

though it chafes our palms,
though arm and shoulder muscles strain
enough to make the crossing a struggle,

enough to make lungs burn
and speech shatter, grunting
as we inch forwards, suspended

in an inarticulate now. Behind us,
the words we have left on the shore
like ownerless clothes.

Before us the heave to the other side,
terra firma, the hope of a new tongue,
the anchored tug and its cargo.

Aulis Monologues

By blood we live, the hot, the cold
To ravage and redeem the world:
There is no bloodless myth will hold.

'Genesis', GEOFFREY HILL

Sacrifice contains an element of mystery. And
if the pieties of classical humanists lull our
curiosity to sleep, the company of the ancient
authors keeps it alert.

'Violence and the Sacred', RENÉ GIRARD

Chorus

The scene is set for war.
The Greek fleet anchored at Aulis
ready to sail for Troy,
the harbour stilled in a breathless awe
even the gods seem to share –
all the gods but one. In spite, not awe,
unforgiving Artemis has withdrawn
her favour so not a breeze stirs the shore.
The vanity of a cuckolded husband
demands the public stage of war
so the Greeks will pursue Helen
to persuade the world of Menelaus' outrage.
But without wind, the performance cannot begin.
Anchors will not be raised nor armies engage;
instead men sharpen their weapons, scratch
and stretch in boredom while they wait to sail.
The first victim of this war will die here, today.
No soldier but an unarmed girl,
Agamemnon's first-born, given in exchange
for Artemis to blow into their sails
and send them on their way;
even for the gods a bizarre piece of trade.
If we thought for an instant her death would save
the life of any young Greek man
or save one Trojan woman from rape and slavery
it would bring some comfort, but her blood
on the altar will be the trickling stream that swells
till her father's house and all in it are swept away.
The wind purchased by this death will be foul,
foul as the tall pyre of corpses that will wait
for the torch on the shores of Troy.

Footsoldier

Blame is a coin passed down from hand to hand:
it starts off hidden in the fists of powerful men
but like most things they want to be rid of
it finds its way down to the likes of us.

I'll give you an example. Helen takes off with Paris
  — good riddance I've heard some say —
but her husband, a powerful man, gathers the lords
and all their ships, all prepared for war
when out of nowhere an eerie stillness descends.
We wait. Temperatures rise. Supplies run down.
We wait some more. The men wager and squabble.

Nature won't comply so Agamemnon sends Calchas
to go find out the gods' true intentions.
The priest comes back with sly and sinister counsel —
Artemis bears a stubborn grudge, he says,
there'll be no wind till Agamemnon pays a price
with his own kin.
                   I'll grant you
it's not a choice a man would ask to face,
but it was clear to all of us which way it would go:
Agamemnon was already itching to get out of Aulis,
in his own mind he'd waved to his family on the quayside,
he was miles out to sea and sailing for Troy.

Next thing we hear is the officers' sour muttering,
'Years of loyal service… no thanks… badmouthed
on the eve of a campaign', while Calchas drip-feeds
hints in high places, 'the men couldn't be trusted,
the anger meant for Troy could climax too soon,
all that frustration spurting out prematurely. Who knows?
They could even harm their own people.'
As if we couldn't tell friend from foe.

In the end it wasn't us who harmed our own
but Agamemnon. He had to pass on the blame
of course, couldn't shoulder it alone.
So the coin passed down, hand to hand.
It was tarnished by the time it came to us, the rank and file.
It always is. It turned our fingers black.

Iphigenia

He wasn't going to tell me.
It was my mother's servant came to us,
the toothless old man I passed in the hall.
I could barely make out what he was saying
his accent was so thick but I heard two words
                    Iphigenia… sacrifice
saw my mother's face flush for a moment
then turn the colour of a seasick recruit.
She listed as if a wave had struck,
repeated the words and the sheer dread
in her voice churned in my gut,
spread up my spine and down my legs
so I couldn't feel my hands or feet.
I heard myself squeak
                    He's lying
but she didn't answer.
Then my father came, still no answer,
he was looking at my mother, not at me
and then I read it in his eyes:
                    Die?

And for what?
So Helen could be brought back?
She doesn't even want to be here.   .
On my knees, begging him to let me
go on being what I've always been,
his daughter.
                    Why does it have to be me?
                    Why not Helen's daughter?
                    Why not Hermione?
Not a word.

He was still looking at my mother, or at his feet.
I looked at his sandals, they were clean,
they were always clean…
I was sure there was something
he wasn't telling us,

48

Someone has a hold over you
someone is making you do this
but he didn't flinch,
his face a mask.

I never knew real fear till then, the urge to flee.
I said terrible things, begged him to hide me away
in a goatherd's hut on a hill,
Is there not one small place for me
in all the territory you command?
dress some slave girl in my clothes
and send her to the altar in my place,
confound the gods if that's what it would take.
Am I ashamed? No.
Fear is stronger than shame.

Then he cried silently
though his tears weren't for me.
He showed me no pity
but kept it to anoint himself,
Agamemnon, once my father,
My whole life, a lie
and then he left.

His guards will soon be back.
My poor mother,
her tears could drown us all.
I have none left.
Fear is stronger than grief.
My eyes are full of sand;
my mind cold as a desert at night.
I see her now like a broken mosaic
with lots of pieces missing,
something from a distant past
and I know the readied knife
has already severed me
from everything I loved.

Will you lie awake tonight, Agamemnon?
How will you remember me
as you toss and turn?
Fresh-
skinned and smiling
as I ran to hug you every morning?
Frail
as any girl
though we used to arm-wrestle
and you would feign defeat?
Proud
as the daughter of a king should be,
believing myself loved and cherished?
Virgin
and humiliated in my girlish innocence,
believing the pretence of a match never made?
A corpse
stripped of parents, siblings, husband, children,
sky, sun and sea
all in the time it takes to draw a breath,
one final breath?

Will you watch as the priest draws his blade across my throat?
Will you hold me down like a dumb animal,
feel the rush of warm blood on your clean skin and clothes?
You might as well. Your hand is on every other part of this.

Clytemnestra

What happened, Iphigenia?
You came out fighting, instinct primed and at full throttle,
threw yourself at your father's feet, arms around his legs
and begged for recognition, for mercy, for your life.
What made you change course from the fight to survive
to this listless resignation? Not the whims and whingings
of Agamemnon's squaddies, steaming and mutinous in their tents,
spoiling for a piece of action. Was it Odysseus,
that fraud, harping on and on about Greek glory
as though your death served some great cause?
The only cause he serves is his own ambition.
Or that pious old snake, Calchas, the priest?
He dropped the poison in your father's ear:
how to appease the goddess and gain fair winds,
kill two birds with one stone, kill two birds
and still your fluttering heart.

Dry-eyed, you watch me weep.
We both know the gods have little interest in my tears
but that won't stop me plaguing them, beating
at their doors with my prayers and offerings.
I gave you a name that means strong-born
but what strength is there in this silence?
Hold tight onto life, don't make it easy for them.
I'd rather you kick and scratch at their eyes,
swear and curse their houses with foul obscenities
than surrender your last moments to this mute compliance.
Fight them, child, don't let them dignify this slaughter
with the pretence of your consent.

Achilles

Shame.
That was the first time in my life I'd felt it.
When her mother looked at my scabbard
then looked me in the eye
my cheeks flushed like a boy's.

At first I didn't believe it when they told me
I was a pawn in Agamemnon's plot.
He promised me as bait to lure his daughter to Aulis,
dangled me there like some kind of trinket
and now she and her mother were on their way
in a flurry of wedding plans and giddy girl-servants.
I was speechless. That was another first.

When Clytemnestra found out the truth
she brought the girl to me. She was so small,
wrists so bird-boned I couldn't take my eyes off them;
a man could circle them both with one hand.
I gave my word: I wouldn't let them go through with it.
But the will of a god is the sharpest blade a leader wields
and he had it all figured out. 'It wasn't my idea', he said,
'it was what She demanded.' Artemis would have Iphigenia
in payment for a slight, and nothing, but nothing else
would raise those anchors or steer those ships out of Aulis.

Well, you know how these things go, and so do the men.
What did they care, after all, for a slip of a girl
when all the riches of Troy were out there waiting for them?
All they needed was a fair wind. In their minds' eye
they already saw themselves returning, cloaked in victory spoils,
rhymed into heroes for the people's ears, welcomed into warm beds.
'What's wrong with you anyway?' they jeered,
'lost your appetite for a fight? Love-sick for Agamemnon's child?'
They got a laugh out of that.
So I gave up and my oath slid back into its scabbard, limp.

Her mother came again, still pleading.
I told her straight: it was out my hands, there was no turning them.
That's when she looked at me like that.

I half expected her to spit.

Chorus

The playwright dresses up trauma as a patriotic spectacle.
Look at Iphigenia, he says — her back to the wall,
see how she makes a virtue of necessity,
not like that pathetic wretch you see in other plays,
dragged screaming to the altar, robes rent by the wind.
Not here, he says. Here, Iphigenia undresses herself
of parental kisses and the promise of a marriage bed
to embrace the greater glory of Greece.

Well, well. Sometimes a writer's back is to the wall.
You knew where the story had to go
so why meddle with convention?
Why risk the mutinous response of a public
as restless as Agamemnon's men?
You played it safe, Iphigenia plays the martyr and obeys.

The scholars say you never finished the play,
that your son or someone else wound it up,
saw there was only one way out for all of you,
marshalled reinforcement from the goddess —
Artemis's *dea ex machina* — that old turn,
suspend a knife in mid-air, switch a doe for a girl,
save Iphigenia's neck and your popularity.

So tonight, once again,
she will thread flowers through her hair,
        dress in her whitest robes
                and we will watch
                        hearts in mouths
                                as she climbs the altar steps.

Euripides

We all know the girl is blameless — whether she meets the knife
in terror or patriotic fervour is hardly the point —
she's the goat Agamemnon sacrifices to escape his own obscurity.
Of course he calls it sacred rite, that's how the magic works:
all that violence is channelled into one staged act.
The men buy into it too. They know a soldier's fate is sacrifice
and sooner or later they too will pay that price.

The public don't like too much meddling with their myths.
You think I haven't tampered with the plot?
Go back and watch again, I expect you'll find
that no-one in this play believes
a god demands the murder of a girl.
And yet a father, driven by ambition, blind,
kills his wife's offspring for a second time.

You think the girl looks powerless, resigned?
Well, who would choose such a way to die?
So we sell it as a youthful ideal of the greater good
but you call that denial. Would you rather see her dragged
by soldiers to the altar, hear her ear-splitting screams
as she begs again for her father to spare her?

Maybe I've seen enough pointless killing in my time.
The ending's not what I'd have wanted, I'll grant you that.
Maybe he didn't take any risks. Maybe I was just old and tired
but divine intervention's a pretty safe card.
The fact is, when a story leads to such a cruel cul de sac,
sometimes magic is the only way out.

Agamemnon

Magic or moral high ground?
Time you made your mind up, playwright.
You want to keep the crowd happy
and still make them think for themselves,
so you knock them out with your gimmicky goddess
and expect them to go home debating
the deeper moral lesson of the tale.

You dress me up as the villain of the piece
who'd slay his own child for blind ambition.
Not so blind. I've seen more blood than I'd like
but try as you might with your weasel words
to make the public hate me, they understand
better than you what it is I have to do.
They know what happens to a conquered people
and they don't want it for their own.
So Calchis comes up with the perfect plan
that lets them off the hook: I let my child die
so they don't have to.
                    Child-killer?
Yes, I killed Clytemnestra's first son.
The people know that and still they play along,
wave me off to war from the harbour wall,
me and every other soldier Greece will spew out
on seas, on plains and onto the pages of plays;
anything to keep the barbarian at bay.

Iphigenia Unwritten

How can I tell/ untell you, father, the pain of Aulis?
Unfathered and unbetrothed/ in one day love's un-pairing/
unmothered and unbrothered/ ungendered and undoweried
by your hand/ beaten down to the price of a beast/ bought
for sacrifice at market on your way to the temple./ Your moment
of momentous denial my undoing / a switch-flicking instant
in your mind/ my down-counted un-minuting with every
heartbeating foot-step to the altar/ fear's dawning
that dusked all affection/ twilighting memory/ pulse-roar
in my ears deafening./ Sun-blinded/ I held fast/ Saw the knife/
closed my eyes for the death-cut/ but waiting turned to
unwaiting/ pulse in my ears to cloud-parting wind/ bright gale
of Her presence/ swept up, stolen/ the beast battered
for this death/ not dead but absent./ Elsewhere
not Aulis/ Where?

        How can I speak/ unspeak
to you/ from this place of not being?/ Undaughtered
by your purpose. Saved by a goddess/ enslaved on unknown
shores. Did you think/ She could be so cheaply bought?/
What can be said/ unsaid of Aulis? Unfinished and unauthored
my story half-way through/ placed in the hands of an apprentice/
unwritten the crushed aloneness/ my walk to the altar/ erased all
in a flashy/ theatrical trick on the stage of war.

Unbleeding pain/ your blood coursing in my veins still
worse than death./ I would welcome Aulis now/
the kind uncoupling knife.

Tuning In

… music is a glass-house on the slope
where the stones fly, the stones roll.

And the stones roll right through
but each pane stays whole.

'Allegro',
TOMAS TRANSTRÖMER

Pórtico da Gloria

I

TUNING IN

In the Pórtico da Gloria
sculpted musicians are tuning up.
Some absently, lost in contemplation,
heads cocked as though listening to
another song inside. Others, mid-chant,
lean towards the pillar on their left
as if to crack a joke with an old friend.
Fingers move independent of eyes,
responding to the string's tension,
teasing it up or down with a subtle whine.

In gatherings at the village hall
when pipers get in tune to play together
it's not the pipes alone they have to hear
but one another, ears primed to heed
the mood of voices in the room, squealing
children in the square outside, the elderly couple
who rise from their plastic chairs
at the first notes of a *pasodoble*
to meet in familiar, formal embrace,
      hand on shoulder
hand on back
      hand in hand
   and dance.

II

THE LAST JUDGEMENT

'...the twenty-four elders fell down before the Lamb, each holding a harp, with golden flasks full of incense, which are the prayers of the saints; and they sang a new song.'

(Apocalypse 5.8)

Only the most fortunate of souls will be saved,
led by the hand or borne up in the arms of angels
to be crowned and take their place among the saints.

The master carved them as children, mere tots.
A little girl clutches at an angel's skirts, shrinks
in terror as demons coil around the pillar below.

Over the great tympanum
the elders play a silent canticle in stone
and guard the faithful's prayers in small vials.

III

The Piper's Apprenticeship

For Xan Silvar

By sixteen he already understood
the piper rarely calls the tune alone,
that each occasion has its proper song
and even though his repertoire was broad
the right one couldn't always be foretold.

He learned he had to tune in on the day
to the frequencies of people, mood and place,
to ornament with discretion, humour, grace;
learned to take his cues from a roman bridge,
the wolf's chestnut grove, a mountain ridge.

On feast-days he took to the roads
sweating in his piper's woollen hose
but with puff to pipe ten kilometres or more.
Or perched, precarious, on the back of a tractor,
pipes squealing with the jolt of every pothole.

Made welcome by every woman of the house
he learned the perils of a host's giving hand,
the art of staying sober without giving offence;
learned to comment on the heat of the day,
the dryness of his mouth and his eagerness

to sample cool, spring water from the well.
He drank deep. Then after rest there would be talk
of weather and corn, and mischief-making rumour
of the priest's child the far side of the hill.
And he learned to gift time and to listen.

The day a neighbour met him on the road
to say a house was recently bereaved
he learned no tune would fit the pulse of grief,
but left his pipes to rest beside the door
and stepped into the darkened, silent room.

Disiparmonio

In a camp for displaced people, children are making music
with hybrid rhythms from mountain to plain, ocean to ocean:
cumbia, salsa, vallenato, bambuco.

They have no male flute to call to the female,
kuisi bunsi to kuisi signi, but the children know
that songs are sleeping all around them.

So they strip the plastic casing from electric cables
and punch holes in it to make a whistle,
beat tin cans into cymbals, scour re-cycling centres

for heat dissipaters to craft a *disiparmonio*.
The children of no-land are forging their own traditions,
taking the heat out of the past.

Santa Fe de Antioquia

In the woods there are butterflies bigger than birds.
Their white and yellow wing-flap slow and silent
above the sun-spattered forest floor.

In old patios there are birds smaller than butterflies,
glints of emerald suspended in a halo of wing-whirr.
Their syringe beaks sip and sip again,

take so little,
demand so little of the world.

Mariel

What happens in the moment between ignorance and grief?
The heart's marimba doesn't miss a beat,
mid-swell or ebb, keeps its own inner rhythm.

That unremarkable moment between innocence and knowing,
before the bitten apple is thrown in dismay,
before loss and the steep descent into pain
are marked by a long legato, the cello's drawn, deliberate bow.

The Dual Citizen

*Whatever pain achieves, it achieves in part through
its unsharability... Physical pain is language-destroying.
Intense pain is world destroying.*

'The Body in Pain', ELAINE SCARRY

The Dual Citizen

*Everyone who is born holds dual citizenship, in the
kingdom of the well and in the kingdom of the sick.*

Susan Sontag

Warm assault of forgotten smells.
An antiseptic tingle in the nose,
the vaguely chemical residue of bleach
ignites memory faster than speech -
who you were
before you first walked through these doors
who you became and
who you ceased to be
in that year of onerous citizenship.

You find you feel at home
knowing enough of the lingo
to get by and not look a fool,
knowing how to play that part -
how to be the good patient,
take your medicine,
observe routine.

For the next thirty-six hours
you step back into that other self,
become again one among the sick,
recall how it feels to be lucky
                    or blessed.

Taxol

So here it comes. Hooked up
with line and catheter to my bruised arm.
I take my medicine, trust

in the yew tree and its venomous balm
that purges cell, soul, self; choose to believe
its flaming torch will guide me through the dark.

I'll hew from it a longbow with the reach
to send a poisoned tip to the cell's root,
hear the twang and shudder when it meets

its mark. Or carve from its russet heartwood a lute
to play when they bind me to a severed bough
and I lie on *Samhain* fires of sacred wood

with willow, hazel, alder, birch and rowan,
till the heat of scorching string, flesh and wood
crack open the bone-vibrating sound

of its ritual song, and I am yew-burnt,
yew-red,
new.

Pain has a shaved head

and no eyebrows. It stands on one leg,
one foot, the side of one foot,
afraid to take up too much space,

knows the meaning of nothing
and the provisional nature of everything,
knows in a split second it could plunge into something worse

but has no tongue to cry out, only a beak that opens
and closes without sound. The soles of its feet are charred,
toenails thick as claws and a grey-green mould

grows slowly up its legs to bloom in the moist places
of the groin and under arms. Spasms
contort the torso into impossible forms

but its eyes never leave the pitiless ground
that thrusts frangipani, oleander, passiflora,
bird of paradise, hibiscus and royal palm

up and up, relentless,
till the nerve-ends of fronds
touch blue sky.

The Very World

Ahmed Catrada never told if he got sick
on the boat to Robben Island,
or if he'd found his sea-legs by the time
he left eighteen years later.

He spoke of the absence of children.
The need for a child's voice so acute
there were days his eyes stung
with the ache to hear a baby cry.

When finally a little girl climbed into his lap
he could not speak, but closed his eyes
as the wave of lost years broke over him
and he fought for breath,

her spindly arms around his neck
a life buoy and a noose of trust.

All God's Children

I used to think I was found.
For years that's what I believed
till one day Martha, a scullery girl, let it slip
– her tongue being as like to slip
as a pair of worn soles on wet cobbles –
not in malice, mind, she only spoke the truth.

Turns out some of us aren't foundlings after all.
My mother, God help her, stood in line in a parlour
with me in her arms, week in week out,
eyes fixed on the ballot till finally a white ball rolled
and gave me what she couldn't: a clean bed,
three meals a day and my three rs.
All I have of her is this blue button
she tucked into the hem of my blanket.
Matron saved it all these years.

Every Sunday fine ladies in fine hats
come to watch us eat our dinner.
Mr Handel says we're all God's children.

Mothwing

In memoriam Tom Cunningham

Sunlight through stained-glass windows
paints coloured planets on the walls.
Restrained notes resonate in the solar plexus.
Words gather in the fragments of a life.

The casket lifts like a boat. Three sons, the bearers,
are borne up today by a shared past and by love,
the oarsman who looks back to where he has come from,
who advances with his back to the unknown.

Beneath a pew the wings of a moth pulse
faint as the fall and rise of a breath
when the beloved's breast is a battered hull
cast adrift in a hospital bed.

Too much to ask: the devotion of a body
to one barely attainable act.
Unobserved, the wings have closed.
When I look down the moth is still.

What happens in that moment beyond witness,
what constellations dissolve and re-form?
Will memories, relentlessly forgotten,
reassemble, fully restored?

Notes

Apples Sweeten in the Dark (p19): The title is taken from Eavan Boland's poem 'This Moment' from *In a Time of Violence* (Norton, 1994).

The Injured Past (p27): The quote from French artist Georges Braque (1882-1963), is used by Anne Cadwallader in the Introduction to her book, *Lethal Allies* (Mercier, 2013) which documents the events alluded to in this sequence of poems, among many others that took place in mid-Ulster in the period between 1972 and 1977.

Standing Ovation in 'The Crum': The Crumlin Road Gaol in Belfast opened in 1846 and served as a fully operational prison for 150 years, closing in 1996. An estimated 25,000 people were imprisoned there during its history. From 1971 many were interned without trial or detained on remand of sentence. In 2012 the building underwent restoration and is now a tourist attraction in the city, hosting tours, concerts and other events, including the exhibition of antique Bolshoi costumes in 2014.

Aulis Monologues (p45): More than one version of the story of Iphigenia's sacrifice survived the oral mythic tradition. In one, she is sacrificed by her father to Artemis. In another she is transported by the goddess to Taurus, on the Black Sea. Euripides' *Iphigenia in Aulis* was first performed in 405 BC and dramatizes the latter version. Probably written in the last years of his life, it is generally assumed that Euripides died before its completion and that it was finished by his son and/or others.

The *Pórtico da Gloria* (p63) is the triple-arched portico of the Romanesque facade of the Cathedral of Santiago de Compostela, reputedly designed and carved by twelfth century architect and stonemason known as El Mestre Mateo.

Disiparmonio (p67): A disiparmonio is an improvised name in Spanish given to a musical instrument made from heat dissipaters. *Kuisi bunsi* and *kuisi zigni* are traditional Colombian flutes. There are male and female versions of the kuisi. The female *kuisi bunsi* has five holes; the male *kuisi zigni* has two.

Mariel (p69) is the title of a piece by Argentinian composer Osvaldo Golijov in memory of his friend Mariel Stubrin. 'I attempted to capture that short instant before grief, in which one learns of the sudden death of a friend who was full of life: a single moment frozen forever in one's memory, and which reverberates through the piece, among the waves and echoes of the Brazilian music that Mariel loved.'

All God's Children (p77): The Foundling Hospital was established in London by philanthropic sea-captain Thomas Coran in 1741. As demand for places grew, infants were admitted through a system of balloting that used red, white and black balls. George Friderich Handel's involvement began when he directed a performance of his *Messiah* there in 1750 and was elected a Governor of the Hospital.

The Very World (p76): The title of the poem is taken from William Wordsworth's *The Prelude*, X1:

> Not in Utopia, subterranean fields,
> Or some secreted island, Heaven knows where!
> But in the very world, which is the world
> Of all of us, the place where in the end
> We find our happiness, or not at all!

Photograph by Peter Harkin

LORNA SHAUGHNESSY was born in Belfast and lives in Co. Galway, Ireland. She has published two poetry collections, *Torching the Brown River* and *Witness Trees* (Salmon, 2008 and 2011), and her work was selected for the *Forward Book of Poetry*, 2009. She is also a translator of Spanish and South American Poetry. Her most recent translation was of poetry by Galician writer Manuel Rivas, *The Disappearance of Snow* (Shearsman Press, 2012).